Heaven is My Google Search

by
Bob Buchanan

Cover design by Vinnie Corbo
Cover photo by Bob Buchanan
Author photo by Natalya Rodriguez
Edited by Vinnie Corbo

Published by Volossal Publishing
www.volossal.com

Copyright © 2023
ISBN 979-8-9877903-6-6

This book may not be reproduced or resold in whole or in part through print, electronic or any other medium. All rights reserved.

Table of Contents

Forward	5
Preface	9
Introduction	11
Mothers	15
Husbands and Fathers	31
Children	41
Musings	63
The Life of a Caulbearer	79
About the Author	117

Forward

I was introduced to Bob Buchanan about a dozen years ago through a mutual friend. I knew very little about Bob, except that he was a very talented photographer and that he used to be a police officer. Right off, I liked Bob's candor, offbeat sense of humor and his no-nonsense style.

Soon after we met, Bob asked me to edit his first novel, *The Lunch*, a captivating love story that transcends space and time. I was surprised that such a tender, in-depth tale was written by a man—especially a hard-boiled ex-cop. But I would quickly learn that a lot about Bob was surprising.

As he and I worked closely together, I discovered that Bob was a caulbearer or medium. Of course, I was skeptical, as many are. But then, my deceased parents began "visiting" Bob when he least expected it—in the shower, trying to have a quiet cup of coffee.

Unprompted, unasked, Bob told me things about my parents and our relationship that he couldn't possibly have known.

"Did your dad chase you around the house when he played with you as a kid?" Bob wondered.

A chill prickled my spine. How could Bob know that Dad used to chase my sister and I around the house, to our delight, pretending to be Quasimodo? How could he know that my mother passed due to sepsis, which Bob interpreted as "something in her abdomen." And how does Bob know that I worry so much…about everything?

So, instead of doubting, I listened.

Bob's visions were particularly active when I went through a cancer diagnosis in 2013. My parents came to him often, demanding that he tell me not to be afraid, that I would be fine. That I would live to see my son graduate high school and college. (I have.) That I would live to hold his children in my arms. (Still waiting on that one…he's only twenty-three.)

When the pandemic was at its height, Bob reached out to me again. This time, it was when a friend died alone in her apartment from Covid 19. After not hearing from Lynn for days, I sent the authorities to do a wellness check and found her there, dead. By my posts online, Bob knew I was troubled by this but received messages from Lynn that she was in a better place and at peace, that I did much more for her than most. Bob's words gave me closure and peace as well.

My ancestors came to Bob again several years later, after my second cancer diagnosis in 2019. He assured me that I would survive this too, even though it would be rough. The treatment put me in the hospital… twice. But here I am, more than two years later, writing the Forward to this book.

Through his other works—*They Speak Through Me* and *I Can't Find You a Boyfriend…or Your Keys: My Life as a Caulbearer*—Bob has given countless examples of how he has touched the lives of others. He's helped solved crimes. He's given grieving mothers solace through his visions. I've read his books with awe and amazement.

Recently, Bob steered a client to me, a woman who lost her son to an accidental overdose and was steeped in sorrow. Bob told Carol that she needed to do something to honor Jeremy—and she did. Writing a book about her son's life—and death—gave her closure and a purpose. It gave her a will to help others and go on with her own life.

This is what Bob does for so many people—offers them peace, answers, closure. I'm proud to call him a friend. I'm astounded by his gifts. His books are his legacy.

The value of Bob's caulbearing abilities are indescribable—whether they bring solace to a Stage 4 cancer patient or bring closure to a parent who has lost a child or to a little girl mourning her beloved goldfish. I guarantee that you will never look at birds, butterflies or flickering lights the same way again. They are all signs from beyond.

- Catherine Gigante-Brown, Author
October 2022

Preface

The title of this book was inspired by one client who, after his session, spoke with the person who referred him to me and said, "I think he Googled me."

He isn't the only one. I do hear that from time to time. When this happens, I have to remind my client that I never asked for their last name. So how would that be possible.

The referring client reminded him of that and asked how I could possibly Google him without his last name.

If you don't believe me try it yourself. Google Jim or Judy or your own first name and see what comes up. Good luck with that.

I do that on purpose. Since many television mediums are being exposed for looking into people who will be on the show, people are skeptical. I am good with that. You will read about this further into the book.

I have also changed what I put in this book a bit from the last two. In the last two, the sessions I did dominated the content. While I do have several sessions in here, I also talk more about what I get and how it works for me; basically, some insight into me, if you will.

Heaven is my Google Search - It's the messages that come from the souls that *are* the messages. I have to rely on *them*. I can't remember what I give people because it comes through me from the other side. That is a good thing because I am lazy. I don't want to have to Google and memorize all that.

I, unlike the television mediums, could not allow myself to hurt people. I just couldn't live with myself. Plus, I would have to remember what I read when in fact I can't remember what I had for breakfast. I have too much going on.

Hell, I would have a lot more money by cutting corners. But integrity is what is important in this modality. These gifts are granted by God. I'm just not willing to take the chance of crossing him. I'm trying to soften the blow when it is *my* time to leave this world. Perhaps, just perhaps he will have some mercy on me.

Introduction

There are a few things that are consistent during my sessions;

One is; Grandmothers make it easier on me, which I both need *and* appreciate, by showing me themselves in the kitchen.

I was working in a real-estate agency doing photoshoots of the agents. When we were scheduling the dates, I told them that weekends were booked because I was doing caulbearer sessions.

I had met with three women who were principals in the agency. As they walked me out, they asked if I could give them messages.

I explained that I would need to sit and go into my zone in order to concentrate. But with that said, just as I was walking out the door, I had a man with me.

I turned around, walked back into the agency and told the women that I had dad with me. He wanted them to know he was there.

At that point, I assumed the message would be for only one of them.

One woman began to cry and ran out of the office. I felt bad but assumed she was the daughter of this man. I looked at the other two and they informed me they were all sisters.

They explained that the one who ran out had just had a child and she wondered if their dad knew.

I gave them some messages from their father and was leaving again when suddenly I had a grandmother with me.

I turned to the receptionist and said, "I'm with a grandmother that is short, fat and in the kitchen with a lot of food."

From what I told her, it made sense to her. She was close to her grandmother. I gave her a few messages and left. This is one of the very few times I did what I call, "the blind side."

After I left, one of the agents in the office said to Carol, "Aren't *all* Italian Grandmothers short fat and cook a lot?"

I was astounded at the ignorance of that woman, but I get this from time to time.

When Carol told me this, I explained to her that: One, I had no idea she was Italian. Two, my mother and her three sisters were all grandmothers, Italian, thin and on the tall side. And three, they rarely cooked. I don't do stereotypes.

Not all grandmothers are kind and compassionate. I have done sessions where I have had both grandmothers who have hated kids or did things to their grandchildren that are mind-boggling.

I know the people who want to prove us fake point to things and say, "Well, it's only a fifty percent chance what we tell people is true."

I have had people book sessions simply to try to prove that point. I just ignore them. I used to not charge them but now everyone pays, no matter what.

When I do my sessions, I only get one to five souls. Sometimes I get more, but too many will get confusing for my client. The souls that come through will be those closest to my client; the ones watching over them.

Very often one soul will take the lead when that occurs. It's the soul my client wanted to talk to. My sessions are always different and always tailored for my clients giving them what they need at that moment. Once the messages they need to hear are conveyed and the window is closed, I will ask them at that point in the session if they have any questions.

This is the point in the session where I am comfortable that the client has gotten what they needed and they told me nothing. Prior to this point, I want the client to only the answer questions I asked with, 'yes, no, or maybe' and *not* expand.

The one question I ask almost every time is, "Does this make sense to you?"

It's important that my clients know they didn't tell me anything.

The souls open a window into my client's life. They tell me what they want my client to hear. I am simply the vehicle they chose to trust with those messages.

Mothers

Elizabeth's Mother's Ring

I met Elizabeth in the park by the Hudson in Peekskill, NY for a session. Her messages came through strong and fast. Elizabeth's mother was the dominant soul. She was strong with a sense of humor. When a soul dominates, it's usually the soul my client is looking to connect with the most. Although it's not always the case, in some instances it is how they were here. In Elizabeth's case, her mother was who she wanted to hear from.

It had been so long since I did that particular session, I had forgotten what messages she received. I often forget the messages as they only travel through me.

At the end of my sessions, I always ask my client if they have any questions. Sure enough, Elizabeth had a specific one. She asked if I knew the location of her late mother's ring.

Really? Hell, I can't find my own stuff half the time! As stated in the title of my last book, I can't find you a boyfriend or your keys. I told Elizabeth I doubted it but I will see.

Elizabeth told me the family checked everywhere but couldn't locate it. She asked if I thought the caretaker may have taken it. My first instinct as a former cop was to say, "Yes." I have investigated far too many cases where that was exactly the situation.

Before I could say anything, Elizabeth's mother yelled at me to bring me back to her. She showed me a dresser with two small drawers on top and several large draws on the bottom. She showed me the second small draw and told me the ring was sitting in the back on the right side of that drawer.

I told Elizabeth about the vision. Elizabeth said the dresser I described was in her mother's closet. She told me they checked there closely and it simply wasn't there. I reminded her that 'finding things' was not what I do, but she should consider checking it again.

About three days later, I received a text from Elizabeth telling me they found the ring in that exact drawer. However, it was in the middle, not the back. I was happy she found it and accepted it was in the middle, not the back. I was just happy I saw it at all. What can I say, the souls do the best they can and I left it there; as did Elizabeth.

Two years later, Elizabeth called me again to inform me her dad had just passed and wanted another session.

As we sat for the session and I went into my zone, both her mother and father came through. However, this time her father dominated the session. This was most likely because her father was who she wanted to hear from. When we finished our session, I told her I remembered about the ring and how crazy and rare that was to receive stuff like that. She reminisced how they had checked that dresser thoroughly and it just wasn't there but was grateful to find it.

Then all of a sudden, her mother is with me laughing. Laughing! Her mother revealed that after she told me where Elizabeth should look, she put the ring in that drawer so they could find it. Wow! The ring wasn't there when they initially checked, but mom went there and made sure they would find it. Once I told that to Elizabeth, it all made sense to us.

The lesson here is that souls will sometimes put things where we can find them. Oh yeah, they will also hide things from us letting their loved ones, that are still here, know they are with us.

Yes, the souls are mischievous at times. Elizabeth's mother wanted us to know she was with us. If, for some reason, you feel your house is haunted by evil, it's highly unlikely. My experience has been evil stays in the dark and doesn't come out. Those noises you hear or smells you smell are nothing more than playful souls. Enjoy the adventure they take you on. Be at rest knowing they are always here for us.

I Saw Two Moms

As I started my session with Linda, I had a woman come in. She was on the tall side and thin.

I heard "mom" twice. I asked Linda if that made any sense and she said it did.

I asked Linda if her mother had passed and if my description sounded like her mom. She confirmed that the description fit.

I continued to convey to Linda what her mom was telling me about herself. Her mother told me she was very intelligent but depressed. Her mother also told me that she was a teacher. She showed me yarn and colorful pillows with designs on them; mostly flowers.

This all made sense to Linda. She told me that her mother crocheted and made pillows.

Her mother went on with more messages that also confirmed it was her.

There was also another woman with her mother as well. She was shorter, heaver and blonde.

I asked Linda if it made any sense. Did she have another woman in her life that fit this description? Unfortunately, she couldn't identify who the woman was. The woman wasn't coming through with any messages, so I let it go for the time being.

However, the woman stayed with me. She also said, "Mom." This confused me...which is not a difficult task, believe me.

It was at this point that Grandmother came through. Grandma was in the kitchen as all grandmothers show me. Yes, as I wrote before, grandmothers make it easier on me which I both need *and* appreciate.

They show me one of three things:

A: a lot of food, which indicates they cooked a lot.
B: *some* food, which indicates they cooked to eat.
or
C: they simply stand there with their arms folded, which indicates they only made reservations.

Yeah, not all grandmothers cooked. Some you couldn't get into a kitchen with a team of wild horses.

I should also add here that not all grandmothers were kind and compassionate.

Anyway, I digress.

Linda's grandma told me she was also a teacher, which turned out to be accurate. We also had a few others come in; including her father and an aunt.

Once the souls finished their messages about their life with Linda, they opened the window on Linda's life. This is what the Caulbearer does. It is at this point, and I am certain, that all the information they receive comes from the other side. My client told me nothing but agreed that the messages about her life came from the other side. I asked Linda if she had any questions.

Linda told me she was adopted and wondered if her biological parents could come through.

I concentrated and asked if they were around.

The blonde woman came forward again. I told Linda she was here. Remember, when we began, Linda wasn't able to identify the blonde woman, which isn't uncommon.

But now the two moms thing was starting to make sense. Linda told me her biological parents were married

and she wanted to know why they gave her up
for adoption.

As I asked her biological mom this question, I was expecting to hear they couldn't afford to keep her, but I didn't let that influence where they would take me. While that would be the most logical reason, logic doesn't always apply, so I shut the thought down and listened.

At this point, another man came through saying, "Dad."

Talk about confusing...but hey this whole message thing confuses me.

The man turned out to be Linda's biological father. He was a short heavy-set man. Linda confirmed this.

Linda found out about her biological parents years ago and even knew who they were. Unfortunately, they had passed before she could ask them this question.

Dad did tell me he was a strict disciplinarian. Once I told that to Linda, she told me they were church people and her mom played the organ.

I believe I mentioned something about music in the beginning but I couldn't remember. Hell, I can't remember what I had for breakfast that morning.

When the messages come through me, I don't remember most of them. If someone was holding me by my feet from the edge of a building and told me they would let me go if I didn't remember all the messages, I'd honestly have to say, "Let go."

Anyway...

As Linda was telling me about the organ, I was getting that mom had an affair. I believe it was with the pastor but Linda believed it was another parishioner. I saw a man with a collar which leads me to believe it was the pastor.

The father had found out about the affair. Mom told me she wasn't sure at the time if Linda was her husband's or the man she was having the affair with.

This threw dad into a rage... understandably so.

I was sure Linda was the child of the man married to her mother. He was definitely her biological dad.

I told that to Linda and she told me that she was the spitting image of her biological dad's mom; her paternal grandmother which confirmed she was the daughter of the man married to her mom.

But the big question was: Why didn't her biological parents keep her? Why did they give her up for adoption?

I was told that it was her biological father's decision. It was his way to punishment Linda's biological mom for having an affair.

From what I saw of the biological father, I believe he would have been abusive to Linda had they kept her. He would have never been able to accept Linda with all the uncertainty. That was the personality I saw in that man.

It was clear that Linda's life was much better with her adoptive parents than it would have been if had her biological parents kept her. This gave Linda closure and she felt relief.

I am certain that things happen as they should in this life; no matter what or how hard that is. Don't get me wrong, we have the power of free will and the power to take control over our lives, but it's all part of the path we travel.

Mother's Day

Each Mother's Day, there are a million people on Facebook wishing their moms a very happy Mother's Day. Mother's Day can be a mixed bag of emotions, because for some, it is *not* a day of happiness. If you are one of the lucky ones, it is a wonderful day.

However, we should not forget others who feel lost on this day. There are those for whom this is not a day they can celebrate. I hope I can make some sense and open people to understanding what these mothers go through. This is not meant to be a downer. Please understand that it is to help those of us who are happy to perhaps understand and lift up those who are having a tough time today.

I do sessions for many, too many, mothers who no longer have their children. This is the hardest thing a parent can live with. When I do sessions for someone who has lost a child, it takes a toll on me. This is because there are no words in the English language that can ease the pain of a mother who has lost a child. I am always at a loss for words as a deep pain overtakes me. The only thing I can tell someone is what I see. Children are always in the light with family. They are with us to celebrate this special day and every day. This is not conjecture, it is real. My only regret is I can't take their pain with me as I leave.

Two Mothers Who Lost Children

Recently, while doing sessions at a psychic fair, two women came to have a session with me who had both lost children. The first session was with Margret, a woman who had lost a daughter. After the session, we talked.

Margret told me her friend Kim was upstairs with another medium. She told me Kim had also lost a daughter. Just as she was telling me this, her friend Kim's daughter Jodi was with me.

As Jodi came in, I got a cold feeling with deep pain inside. I knew Kim wasn't going to get what she needed from the medium upstairs. I told Margret if Kim didn't get what she needed, she should bring Kim to me and I would give her a few minutes.

I told Margret to tell Kim not to tell the people at the fair that she was coming down or they would charge her. I also knew from Jodi that Kim wasn't getting any messages and Jodi wanted to talk to Kim. I was also being told Kim would not pay again if the session she had was bad. She wouldn't trust someone else.

About fifteen minutes later, Margret came downstairs with Kim and asked if that offer was still good.

I simply smiled and said, "Of course," and directed Kim to my room.

Within seconds Jodi was talking to me. After all, she was already with me. Jodi told me she had been sick her whole life and life for her was tough. I conveyed Jodi's messages to her mom.

Kim was very appreciative and thanked me. She was very happy Jodi came through. She didn't think she would because the medium she sat with upstairs didn't get Jodi until Kim asked for her.

Now, that in and of itself doesn't mean the medium wouldn't have gotten her. That happens sometimes. For some reason and I don't have an answer for it. But I do know that the souls want to be asked for. However, according to Kim, the medium gave her nothing more than, in her words, funeral-home-speak.

The usual: She is happy. She is in a good place. Etc, etc... Kim was really upset and I didn't blame her.

Before I start a session, I tell all my clients that everyone I get is in the light in heaven and that they are whole again. Later they may show me how they died which is often as important.

The sad thing about this is Kim went to this woman in good faith hoping to talk to Jodi. When that didn't happen, she believed all of us were fake. Thankfully, I was able to restore her faith in us.

I am not supposed to get upset with people who are fakes, but I do. I wish people who do this because they think it's cool or are seeking attention for themselves would stop doing this. They are hurting people and that isn't right.

Sadly, I will say that about ninety-eight percent of people who *say* they have the gift, do not. Often, they actually suffer from mental illness. They rely on the client to talk a lot. If you feel you are with someone like that, get up, take your money back, and leave.

The very same is true for those who have lost their mothers. They are with you and will be watching out for you as they always have.

The Flower Petal

Sometimes I am asked to do a group session with a family. This is called a gallery. At one session, I was with the father, Chris, mother, Anna and daughter, Judy.

Upon sitting down, Chris' father came through right away, as did Anna's mom.

I was giving them the messages from the souls when my attention turned to Judy. I was hearing a little voice saying, "Mommy."

As always, when I hear or see a child my heart drops. When this little girl came through, I asked Judy if she lost a child, hoping the answer was no. She told me yes, not her child, but a child she was very close to. I told her the child was telling me that Judy was like her mom and was very close to her. This turned out to be true.

The session was taken over by the child at this point. Another woman showed up right after her who told me she was her mom's mom who was there for her, along with the rest of the family who first showed up.

After I left the session, Chris reached out to me in a text later and we spoke quite a bit about how the child, Kelly, was happy and at peace. The next morning Kelly was with me giving me more information to relay to her grandparents and Aunt Judy. She was excited and wanted them all to know she is healthy and happy.

When I awoke the next morning at 5am, I went to the kitchen to grab my coffee and saw a pink flower petal in the middle of the floor. It was in great shape. It looked like an Orchid petal, but I wasn't sure. I picked it up and threw it away thinking my wife must have dropped it.

When she came into the kitchen I asked her if she dropped it and she said no but perhaps it came in on her shoe after walking the dog the night before. The petal was in too good of shape for it to have been stepped on. I went into the other room to check my orchids, but none were missing petals.

It was a mystery. I had no idea where it could have come from. And at that hour, I couldn't put two and two together.

It was only later that I remembered that I had awoke at 2am to get some water, and at that time, there was nothing on the floor.

There was no way I could have missed it, even at that hour. Now, as a skeptic, I had explored all avenues of where it would have logically come from.

I continued to ponder how it got there when suddenly I heard Kelly's little voice say thank you.

I reached out to Chris to see if a pink flower petal meant anything to him. He said yes. He sent me a photo of Kelly when she was four wearing a pink dress and holding pink flowers. Pink was her favorite color.

Later that day, I spoke to Aunt Judy and conveyed to her what had happened. She also told me pink was Kelly's favorite color. When she was sick, the neighbors in their neighborhood, including the local fire department, all displayed pink in support of her.

Kelly had reached out to say thank you in a way only her family would know. I spent a lot of that day tearing up with the pain of bringing her through and what she felt for her family.

It is this small flower petal and a child's 'thank you' that makes doing this worthwhile.

Appreciate and Celebrate Your Mothers

Please appreciate your mother on Mother's Day. Unless you are a mother who has given birth or, like Judy, mothered a special little person, you can never fully understand who mothers are or what they go through for us.

All that being said, I hope all mothers have a happy Mother's Day. Don't let sadness overtake you. Reflect upon your life with those who are no longer here. Do not forget your children who are still with us. They need you. Stand tall against the sadness and don't let it defeat you.

Let it, in some way, lift you. I know that is easier said than done but do everything you can to honor your life with those who are no longer with us, whether it be your mother or your child.

    If your mom is still with you, celebrate her with happiness and do not take her for granted. If she has issues, try to forgive her; even for just one day. I know that is a lot to ask, but sometimes forgiveness helps you more than anything else.

Husbands and Fathers

Happy Birthday Pop

My client Judi called to tell me about something that happened in the car while her husband Harold was driving. Their son Alan had passed from cancer. They were absolutely devastated.

Their vehicle has one of those pop-up displays where the GPS and other apps will come up on the screen. During this particular drive, the screen was completely blank when suddenly a message came on the screen.

"Happy Birthday Pop."

It was Harold's 80th Birthday.

Judi asked me if I thought it was a message. Alan was with me and told me it was. There is no doubt about it. I told Judi if the message popped up with a message advertising a car dealership, then no, it wasn't a message.

What made this so important is no one other than Alan called his dad 'Pop.' Yes, Alan made sure his message could not be questioned. Alan's message to his dad was just what Harold needed at the time he received it.

This happens often. We get what we need at the time that we need it. Sometimes we just don't realize its happening. We just have to be open and pay attention to what goes on around us and we will see more.

Always be hopeful never hopeless.

Always stay optimistic never pessimistic.

John Told Me He Would Send Her a Message

I was doing a session with Alice who had just lost her young husband John suddenly. She had never met a medium or anyone like a medium and she was very skeptical.

John came through for her immediately with important messages. Although her messages were strong and very accurate she still wasn't sure about the messages she received. Alice questioned everything and I was fine with that. I understood she wanted to be sure this is real and John was in a good place.

Alice wanted more. She was hoping this would be a biography, but it never is. I can only give a client what the souls give me. I push them, but they are in control of the messages, not me.

John dominated our session which often happens when the person I am speaking with wants to hear from a particular soul. It is important to me to make sure I get as many messages as they will give to help my client to get some peace and, if possible, closure.

That being said, when a client questions everything, it makes it difficult. I always stay with what they give me. It's not like I have a choice.

At the end of our session, I asked John to give me something more for Alice; something she couldn't question.

John showed me a cell phone and told me to tell Alice he would communicate through the phone to her so she would know he is okay. It wasn't exactly what I was hoping for.

John made it clear to me that he was doing things around the house. I repeated what he was telling me. I told Alice she would hear things going on in the house and John would turn lights on and off; perhaps even a TV.

She told me that would scare her. I assured her it would be him and there would be nothing to be frightened about but that didn't calm her down. At this point, John showed me the phone and reassured me that he didn't want to scare her.

When they show phones, I can never know exactly what they will do because there are so many things they do. It could be several different things like:

- talking to us that sounds like choppy static,
- sometimes a voice whispering,
- a ring with no number at all,
- or 000-00-0000

I had a client where a soul sent him and his ex-wife a text while they were texting each other and said he was okay.

Those are a few things that have happened. Even that made Alice a little nervous but he told me his communication would bring her comfort and it wouldn't be scary.

This is where I ended our session; yelling at John in my head that he better do it. Yeah, I do that. I want to make sure they do what they tell me they are going to do. I have to say, they actually do what they say most of the time.

Two days after Alice's session she sent me a text and asked me to call her. When I did, she told me that morning she got a message on her phone that wasn't a normal text. It was not a message from Apple or anyone else.

The text said "Happy Birthday Alice B", with balloons.

She told me her husband John was the only person who ever called her by that name and it *was* her birthday, John didn't forget. As I was talking to her, John showed up, laughed and let me know it was him and that he kept his word.

When I assured her it was him, it brought her comfort. I love it when the souls do what they tell me they are going to do. It may take time but they usually come through.

Always stay hopeful, never hopeless.

Live an optimistic life, not a pessimistic one.

During a Duo

During a Duo (face to face) phone session with Sue, both her mom and dad came through. Dad was the one she wanted to hear from at this point as he had recently passed.

As we started Sue's session, her dog started barking. I was already in my zone. Once I'm in my zone, barking dogs do not bother me. Although I am aware, no matter how loud they are, the volume in my head is turned way down. However, this time the volume grew louder and louder.

Dad told me he loved the dog and was playing with him. I told dad to stop and talk to me. All the while Sue is telling the dog to be quiet. I told Sue the dog will quite down soon and it did.

As we continued with our session, particularly when talking about her dad and her husband, I would hear a male voice confirm what I was saying. For example, when I was telling Sue that her husband and dad were close and that her husband looked out for her dad, she validated it.

But at the same time, I heard a male voice also say, "Absolutely." I simply assumed her husband was sitting listening in and agreeing with what I said. There could be no other explanation. After all, dad was talking to me. The other souls had all been women.

I was also hearing some feedback from my voice but it was obvious what that was. I was sure it was either her husband or son who decided to sit in off camera. At the same time Sue was hearing static, but I was unaware that was happening.

As we finished, dad asked me if it's okay if he plays with the dog again so Sue would know he was there.

I said, "Be my guest."

At the point, I told Sue the dog was going to start barking again dad wanted her to know he was there. Sue chuckled and said that's fine. Then I heard the male voice say, "Good."

After we finished the session, Sue and I were talking. I asked who was there with her. Was it her husband or son?

She told me no one was there in the house. It was at that point when I realized the male voice was her dad coming to me through the phone as well as in my head during our session.

I told Sue what was happening. It made our session more interesting. This has happened on rare occasion before. I wondered if it was because I had my ear bud in. But I had several duo sessions since and there was no static or voices.

I did have some feedback, but that isn't unusual from time to time while talking on the cell phone.

Just as we were about to hang up, I noticed that the dog wasn't barking.

I said to Dad, "So you're going to make a liar out of me with the dog?"

He smiled and sure enough the dog started barking at that point.

I said to Sue, "I thought he was going to make a liar out of me but there it is."

We both got a kick out of that.

Children

The Loss of a Child

Understatement: The most difficult thing I experience when I'm in a zone with a client, is to have a child come through. Their age doesn't matter whether the child is a newborn or sixty. The worst thing that can happen to a parent is losing a child, grandchild, niece, or nephew.

The pain is insurmountable; in any circumstance. That being said, it is slightly more bearable when we watch a child struggle with an illness verses a sudden unexpected passing. Don't get me wrong, nothing is easy. That isn't what I am saying. It's just a little more bearable when watching a child, or anyone, pass who has suffered a long painful illness. There is some solace to see them finally at peace.

When a child is lost, there is always a piece missing in the life of the loved one who lost that child. The loss alters their lives forever. I can talk about it and I understand it to a point. But having never experienced it myself, I can't truly understand it. No one can understand the pain, unless they have experienced it themselves.

I can never find the words I feel I need to give parents relief. I feel impotent and unnecessary. My only hope is to let them know their child is at peace in some way. The child will let me know how that is. When I do,

I push the souls hard to get as specific about the child as the souls allow me to. When I do that, I have been fortunate to get more specifics. This is important to the parent.

I have been blessed to this point and have not suffered a loss of such magnitude. So I can not have a complete understanding of what people go through, only from a distance. One thing I do get from the child that has passed, is to tell their parents not to forget their siblings who are still with them. I only get that when the soul tells me that my client is doing just that.

I will let my client know the wishes of the soul that is with me. I should add here, that I don't just say, "Oh, by the way…"

No, the souls will give me information that they have a brother or a sister who is in some way being neglected. Unfortunately, many do not heed the wishes of that soul and continue to neglect the children that are still here. When we do that, we cause more pain and separation from their family.

That is why it is important we do not lose the connection with our other children. I know it is hard and this is very personal, but we must try to think of the others here and not get lost. They want us to honor them and never forget them. But not at the expense of the surviving siblings. They want us to remember the good times when they were with us and cherish the time we spent together.

I had a client that ignored that advice. She treated her other son like he didn't exist. Now there is a great distance between them and she has lost her other son even though he is still here. Her surviving son has very little to do with her and there is a separation between her and the rest of the family who is also hurting. By driving the family and other loved ones away like that, you end up feeling very alone. Please believe me. They do not want that for you.

At no point in this piece am I saying to forget those who have passed. I would never do that. I am just saying you will do more to honor the souls that passed by finding a way to continue with your life as best you can.

The best advice was from a woman who lost her daughter. She told me it never gets easier just softer. I use that now as it makes sense of a loss that will never get easier.

My Nephew is Missing

On Sunday night, November 13, 2016, I arrived home from a small party where I had several sessions. As normal, I was drained after doing these sessions; especially at a party.

My wife was on the phone with her friend Patricia. She was very upset and asked if I could speak with Patricia and possibly get something for her.

When I took the phone, Patricia told me her nephew Joey was missing. His family had been trying unsuccessfully to get in touch with him all day. She wanted to know if I could get anything on Joey's whereabouts.

As I started talking to her, I explained I was tired but would see what I can get. As I was saying this Joey, came to me. He showed me him lying on a floor unconscious by what looked like a modern coffee table with white powder on it.

I was pretty sure Joey had passed by the way he came to me. But unless there was proof, knowing Patricia as I did, I knew that would put her over the edge and would not have helped her at this point.

Understanding that, I told her about my vision and that perhaps Joey was partying and would show up soon. She told me he never did drugs and that it didn't make sense.

I told her maybe someone else was doing the drugs and he was asleep. I told her I would see what I could get the next day and we hung up.

On Monday, the police found evidence that Joey was murdered. They had three suspects, but Joey's body was missing.

Patricia called me. She was understandably upset with the news about Joey's murder. She asked me if they will ever find his body.

Without hesitation, I said, "Yes, by the side of the road in New Jersey."

I had no idea where that came from or why.

Two days later, on Thursday morning November 16th, I walked into my daughter's apartment. The news was on and a story was playing showing an aerial shot over a tent by the side of the driveway going into a boat yard at the Jersey shore. They discovered it two days after I told Patricia that they would not only find Joey's body, but also were.

I had to sit down; I was so surprised at the accuracy of the statement which just popped out of my mouth.

This does happen on occasion. I shouldn't have been surprised. As the case progressed, Patricia asked if they would arrest the three suspects. I told her they would be arrested and they would be convicted.

Three suspects were arrested. James Rackover and Lawrence DiLione were both charged with murder and Max Gemma was charged with hindering prosecution.

Once Rackover's trial started, Patricia was in touch with me often. The anxiety of this trial had them concerned. Like most trials, it's a roller coaster ride of ups and downs; for both sides.

They were worried he would get off. I kept to the messages I was getting that Rackover would be convicted. I'm sure those messages gave her some comfort but she never expressed that to me.

Rackover was convicted of murdered and received twenty-three years to life; the max NY state law allowed.

DiLione had initially pleaded guilty to murder and manslaughter. The judge accepted the plea but later DiLione attempted to change his plea to not guilty.

This caused anxiety in the family because they worried they would have to sit through another trial. I told Patricia it would not happen and he would have to stand by his plea. And that is what happened.

The family was unhappy that Gemma wasn't charged with murder, but he was convicted of hindering prosecution.

I explained to Patricia that he was giving the police information important to the case. Now, I don't know if that was the case, but it was what was in my crazy head and I have to go with it.

I didn't talk about this case. This is my policy when I work on any high-profile case. I will not watch the news so I am not influenced in any way by what I hear on *this* side.

I have to keep faith in what I am being told. I let the souls guide me. They never let me down.

The reason I am talking about it now is because the television show *48 hours* did an expose' on it.

I am writing this six years after the events above took place. I will admit I do not remember everything I got with this as the messages come *through* me.

That's why I just kept to the highlights.

Fentanyl Poisoning

I was doing a session with Elizabeth. Elizabeth had lost her son Jimmy to what appeared a drug overdose. Many in her family were accusing him of suicide. However, Jimmy let me know in no uncertain terms it was fentanyl. I told that to Elizabeth. She was somewhat relieved but still wasn't sure what she should believe.

About a week after our session, Elizabeth sent me a text letting me know that the medical examiners' toxicology report came in. The results: fentanyl poisoning. This confirmed the message I received from Jimmy. Although this didn't make the passing of her son any easier, nothing could, but it gave her relief knowing that it wasn't suicide nor a drug overdose. This put all the condemnation from her family to rest and allowed her to properly mourn the loss of her son.

Sadly, today I am seeing a lot more fentanyl poising than I have in the past 4 years. I did another session with a father named Martin. He lost his son Chris. I told Martin I was getting a headache which indicates to me that something in Chris's head took him.

The souls chose to give me a headache when it's in the head. When it's anything else, they rub or tap the place on their body that caused their death. They know I hate that but they have a sense of humor and love to bust my chops.

After telling Martin that Chris' passing was an accident and that Chris wanted him to know that, Martin felt some relief. As it turned out, he had a headache and asked his friend if she had any aspirin? Chris' friend gave him what she thought was aspirin, but instead it was a fentanyl tablet.

I wonder if that was by accident? As I write this, I am getting the friend who thought it would be funny to get Chris high at school when this took place. It will not make a difference at this point to tell Martin and will only cause him more anguish. I have to use discretion and spare my client's feelings. If I felt it would make a difference, I would reach out.

Please be very careful with drugs today. There is too much fentanyl out there which adds to the danger of drugs.

Always be hopeful, never hopeless.
Always be optimistic, never pessimistic.

All Goldfish go to Heaven

My client in this case, was a nine-year-old girl named Natalie with whom I am very close.

She called me in a hysterical state crying uncontrollably. The goldfish Goldie she won at a fair about five years earlier had died. Her mom and her attempted to revive her to no avail. She wanted to know if Goldie is okay.

I happened to at an event doing videos of bands when she called, so I had a problem hearing her. I inadvertently called Goldie 'he' instead of 'she.' That made things much worse for Natalie.

I can't tell you how heartbreaking this was for me to see her in such pain over a goldfish. Part of the problem was that she had just come back from spending a week with her dad who is mentally abusive. Unfortunately, the family court doesn't seem to recognize that as an issue.

I told her about my vision, in which was Goldie swimming in a beautiful blue ocean with her mom and friends, and how happy she was to be there. That seemed to work a bit until it came time to bury Goldie at a special place Natalie had chosen.

As we were about to bury Goldie, Natalie had another meltdown. I know this is because of her separation issues. Issues caused by the child advocate in family court when they made Natalie go to her dad every other day at the age of three.

We tried to calm her down but were unsuccessful. I figured it would get a little easier with time. Eventually, she took a vacation with her mom and she seemed okay.

But just the other day, I get a text from Natalie asking, "How is Goldie on the other side? I miss her."

What is the common denominator here? She had just returned from a week with her dad.

I told her, "Goldie is swimming with her friends. She wants you to be happy for her."

She responded, "I am."

I once again told her Goldie is swimming in heaven in a beautiful blue sea with her mom and friends. I am not sure if that helped, but the truth is the vision. And I was seeing was just that. Goldie was swimming in heaven in that beautiful blue sea.

It was an amazing vision. I wasn't just telling this beautiful little girl a lie to make her feel better. No, it became a colorful movie; a vision I have when in my zone.

Yes, it is clear that all goldfish go to heaven. I understand this and I hope Natalie does too.

My Friend was Murdered

On August 4, 2016, I receive a text from a client named Mariella telling me her friend Karina was jogging when she was murdered in Howard Beach, Queens NY on August 2nd. She asked if I would reach out to the family.

I told her 'no,' the family would have to reach out to me. I never reach out to people. They must reach out to me. It's how I work and I know in situations like this one the family would be inundated with calls from people who claim they do what I do and look for an opportunity to become part of the news story.

At this point, I should add that Karina *had* been coming to me because I wouldn't reach out to the family. I suspected the family would also not be reaching out to me. I was feeling Karina's frustration. This caused me to call the police hotline to see if I could talk to someone regarding what I was getting about this homicide. As usual, I was ignored by the police.

It wasn't too long after the initial text from Mariella that she contacted me again; this time by phone.

It was a Sunday afternoon. I was sitting at our town park by the kiddie pool with my family. I moved away from everyone and sat on a nearby bench to speak with her. Mariella informed me that a family cousin was going to call me to check me out to see if I was legit.

While sitting there talking to Mariella on a beautiful sunny day nowhere near water, I felt a water droplet on my right elbow. I thought a bird must have done its business on me, but no, it was water. I let it go.

Within a minute, another droplet hit my left elbow. Again, not a bird. There was simply nowhere those droplets could have come from. Finally, I realized they were tears from heaven. Yeah, I knew it was Karina letting me know she was happy that I would be there for her parents.

Less than fifteen minutes later, a cousin called me to question me about who I was and how I work. As we spoke, I became overcome with emotion and had a tough time talking with her. We finished the conversation by setting up an appointment for me to go out to the home of Cathy and Phil, Karina's parents, the following Tuesday.

Upon my arrival at the Vatrano home, I was greeted by many of Karina's family. This included several cousins and her sister, along with her mom and dad.

After being introduced to everyone, I sat at the table and went into my zone. Karina came through and showed me she was sucker-punched by a dark skin man. She told me she fought back as best she could. I saw his face scratched and thought she got his eye. I told them this man didn't set out to hurt anyone but was extremely angry.

When he attempted to talk to her while she was jogging, she ignored him that angered him more. This is what instigated the attack.

The police were saying she was raped. However, I informed the family she was not but that he did *attempt* to rape her, but was unsuccessful. One of the cousins questioned my accuracy, but I stood strong. That is what Karina was telling me and it is what she wanted her parents to know. I always stand strong when it comes to the messages they give me.

I also told the family that Karina scratched his face. I thought she may have gotten him in his eye but she definitely hurt his hand. I asked if they checked the hospitals and I was advised that the family wasn't sure. The police checked the hospital the next day but the perp had not gone to the hospital at that point.

It wasn't until a few days later that perp had his father drive him to the hospital because his hand was infected from attempting to clean it in a puddle in the park. We later found out that the doctors found her tooth wedged in his hand.

Between August 14 and January 16 of 2017, I was in constant contact with Cathy and Phil; mostly Phil. I told him I saw a two-story garden apartment. Phil sent me photos of people he suspected and photos of garden apartments in the area. I knew Phil was desperate to find the man who took his daughter's life. This was painful for me as well because I didn't get a hit off of any of the photos and I was desperately hoping I would.

Phil was difficult and wanted to believe me, but he would say 'of course' to everything I told him. His assumption being that everyone who experienced what he was experiencing felt the same thing. This is simply not true.

I was sitting on my deck talking to him on the phone when I told him something about Karina's passing and he did it again. I needed to give him something he couldn't pass off as a general statement.

I needed something that would help him understand that the messages came from her. I asked Karina to give me that. At that moment, she showed me a photo of her with their dog. She was holding the dog's head. I told Phil about that photo. Phil told me he would remember a photo like that and the photo didn't exist.

The movie Karina played for me was strong, which means it's not symbolic, it's real. I asked Phil to

please look for it when he gets a chance. He told me
he would.

Well, the next day, I got a text from Phil. It was a
photo of the screen on his laptop. It was the photo I told
him about. I believe that turned things around for Phil.
He could now allow himself to believe in me a bit more.

On the morning of January 16, 2017, while I was
doing my self-hypnosis, a vision came to me of NYPD
cops in a huddle talking in front of Trump Tower. One of
them turned to me and told me that an arrest is coming.
I sent a text to Phil and Cathy. They called me and I told
them what I saw.

Cathy said, From your lips to God's ears."

I said, "It's coming in about two weeks."

On February 4th, my phone blew up with texts at
10:55pm from Karina's friends telling me an arrest was
made. This was slightly over two weeks later.

I avoid the news when I am involved with any
high-profile homicides such as this. When it comes to the
news, there is too much misinformation and I didn't want
anything to take me away from my zone, as I call it.

I turned the news on that evening, just in time for
the perp walk of Channel Lewis. I had told the family
that I felt he would be slow-witted. As I watched, he
turned out to be exactly who I saw.

**One thing I did see that wasn't right, was that he
had blond hair on the top of his head. This was six months
later, so he may have I was never able to confirm that.**

When Phil and I were looking for that two-story
garden apartment and we couldn't connect, I wondered
why I was seeing that apartment building. As it turned
out, he lived in a brownstone building on the second floor.
His mother lived there as well. She had a large garden on
the patio. That may be what I was seeing. I don't always
see things as they are, but I will accept that to a point.

I went to the first trial on March 19th. The
first day, Phil and Cathy asked me if there would be

a conviction. I said that I saw a party celebrating the conviction, but not this time. I told him two jurors were not going to vote for a conviction. I pointed out an African-American woman in a black dress with white polka dots as the leader against conviction. She along with another woman, convinced the jury not to convict because the cops were racist. That jury turned out to be a hung jury.

Several months had passed and I hadn't heard anything from Cathy and Phil. Then I got a sign. However, I didn't realize it was a sign at the time.

I was driving north on the Taconic State Parkway in Yorktown in rush hour traffic at 7pm. I was in the middle lane when all of a sudden something hit my windshield. I thought for a moment I was being shot at. It hit so hard that it actually made me jump.

It turned out to be a redtail hawk that completely covered my windshield. I couldn't see a thing. It seemed like an hour but was only a matter of seconds when the hawk lifted off the windshield and flew away. Not one feather came off that bird. I got out and looked for it.

I thought, 'It had to be dead.' But it wasn't anywhere to be found.

I had no idea if that was a sign or not. I didn't give it much thought. Several weeks later in the middle of the day, I was driving South on the parkway. I was thinking about the second trial and whether it had happened or if it was coming up anytime soon.

So I called Cathy and Phil to ask. They told me they were just about to reach out to me to tell me it was coming up in two weeks. As I was talking to them, another redtail hawk comes straight at me with it's talons out like it was going to grab its prey then flew off at the very last second.

I jumped and they heard me. I told them it was sent by Karina. She is letting me know she was going to get him this time and there would be a conviction.

Now, was that the same hawk? I can't confirm that. However, as I am writing this, that is what I am getting. I believe it was.

I went on the first day of the second trial on March 26th. I was sitting in the courtroom by myself. There were three others off to my right. All of a sudden, I was getting this depressed feeling; a feeling of defeat. It was an 'all is lost' kind of thing. I had no idea why.

In less than a minute, the doors opened behind me and the defense team walked in. It all hit me and made sense in that moment. I knew there was going to be a conviction and they knew it was hopeless. I told Cathy and Phil. This gave them the hope they needed.

As I sat and watched the trial, I looked at the jury to see if I could get something from them. All I was getting was there would be a conviction this time. I told this to Cathy & Phil. They questioned me about one juror in particular. I told them I felt she, herself, had experienced sexual abuse or worse and would not be a problem.

I attended the trial on the last day as well. I left when the judge charged the jury and told them if they didn't have a verdict by 10pm, they would have to continue the next day. This was, if I remember correctly, was around 4 or 5pm.

I couldn't stay for the deliberation as it may have gone to 10pm as the judge mentioned. At 8:17pm, I received a text from Jodi, the cousin whom I asked to keep me informed, saying the jury wanted to see the confession again. I answered her. I told her it was one juror that was holding things up. This juror was questioning the confession and wanted to see it again.

As it turned out, I was correct. I stood firm that there was going to be a conviction. I also believed because of the time, it may have to go to the next day.

About 9:35pm that evening, I got a text from Jodi, "GUILTY!"

I have spoken to Cathy and Phil on occasion since the conviction and went to visit them once. Karina continued to send them messages through me that always made sense including a light that came from Karina's bedroom at night. There was no light turned on at the time. I saw the light as Karina and they confirmed that.

It has been many years now and I only reach out once in a while. Both Phil and Cathy have told me they feel her and are hearing her. I realize I am no longer needed.

Like all parents who have lost children, there will always be a piece missing. But their ability to communicate with them, helps them.

During this whole event, I felt uncomfortable and that perhaps I was in their way. I was told by many that I brought peace to them. I have no reason to doubt that. That is the reason why I do this.

The entire time that this was in the news, I kept out of the limelight. I never talked about it. After the trial, I did start to talk about it a little. However, when Nancy Grace decide to do a show on it, I decided to write this piece.

I will continue to be here for Cathy and Phil. They are special people to me. Karina and her parents will also have a prayer and a special place in my heart for them.

Musings

Hawks

The souls will guide animals and birds to us to let us know they are with us. Although the Cardinal is the more common bird they use, I have had Bluebirds show up where they shouldn't. The newest bird to show up for me is the redtail hawk. When I see the redtail hawk, it usually means things will turn out the way I hoped. I have had a few special interactions with the redtail hawk.

In my last book, *I Can't Find You a Boy Friend... or Your Keys: My Life as a Caulbearer* (page 23), I wrote about a redtail hawk that hit my windshield and flew off without losing a feather about a week later a Redtail hawk came down at my car talons out like it was going to grab a mouse and flew off at the last second. I knew the message it brought me was for the trial of a woman named Karina who had been murdered. The perp was convicted. This is when the redtail hawk first showed up as a sign for me.

Family Court

I had just served my granddaughter's father with an order of protection for my daughter and was hoping this would help protect her.

I was walking in the parking lot toward the courthouse in the city of New Rochelle, when a redtail hawk came flying out of nowhere right over my left shoulder and grabbed a pigeon right in front of me. There were no trees where the hawk came from. I didn't see it sitting anywhere.

Things did go well for my daughter and granddaughter for a while immediately afterward. We are still involved with this custody case, and as of this writing, I have no idea what will happen. I haven't seen a redtail in a while. I am hoping another will show up to give me a sign that things will work out for the best for my granddaughter.

Redtail Habitat

Redtail hawks prefer deciduous forests and adjacent open fields. In Karina's case, that is where the hawks were. But in my daughter's case, it was a city and the redtail is not a city bird. This is why it was significant. It worked for that particular instance.

Since then, the redtail hawk has been showing up for me often. It's usually when I have a situation I am concerned about and wonder what the resolution will be. Things always worked out the way I needed them to. I now consider the redtail hawk to be my power animal. It happens often enough that I have no doubt about the messages they bring.

The Choice is Yours

Every day we wake up we have two choices:
One - decide to make today a good day and find the good in life,
or,
Two - decide this will be a bad day and make no effort to change that.
The choice is yours. No one else. Do not surrender your life to toxic people who may attempt to control you and your life.
Don't get me wrong. You don't have to jump up dancing each morning. Yeah, that would be weird. I have done that — that's how I know. Now, there's a vision you will not be able to get rid of; especially knowing I sleep in the nude!
Try to change how you see things and approach them. My main focus for this piece is for the folks who are in situations and relationships, either work or personal, and believe things will always stay the same.
I have many that share a similar point of view. They believe their life will never change and the way things are today will be the way they will always be.
One client of mine was very unhappy at work, and like most people, she could not change the situation for some time. Her boss had a vendetta against her

because the boss aligned herself with someone who was always trying to interfere in my client's life. My client had that situation under control but it compounded when that person ingratiated himself with the boss and the boss sided with that person.

I told my client that things would change and the boss would see who this guy really was. I got pushback from my client. She said I was wrong and this is the way things will always be. She believed she had to find a new job giving up her many years at the current job and start over somewhere else.

But sure enough, the boss eventually saw who that guy really was and now she is making it up to my client. Things at work got better as I told her they would.

I always try to stay optimistic and realized that today is gonna be a great day for me. How do I know? I just saw Klondike is not going to discontinue the Choco Taco! Yes, this is a good day already.

See, it doesn't take much. Just the little things can make a difference in your life.

Important note: I understand some people experience life-changing events, but this is not what I am addressing. I'm talking about learning to live day to day without projection. Projecting on your life is usually wrong. It can set you up for a bad day or even a bad life.

Fall

As I sit silently on the rocks watching the powerful Hudson River flow in all its glory, wildlife abounds. It depends on the river to provide the essentials of life.

As I watch this wonderful display, I am taken away from the usual thoughts that bind me to my day allowing me to let go, relax, open my mind and listen to the sounds of the music nature provides me at this moment.

As I drift away, I look up noticing the beautiful fall leaves backed up by a deep blue sky displaying themselves in bright yellows, oranges and reds. As this magnificent view takes me away, I am saddened at first that it will only be a few days before the dying leaves will drop in all their glory, leaving the way for renewal next year.

My mind, as it often does, takes off to thoughts from who knows where? Is this a message? Why isn't it until their life is over that they display such beauty? What message are they conveying?

Only moments into this wonder, I suddenly realize what the message is: Death isn't dark. It isn't final. It continues in a bright beautiful colorful way.

Only those who can understand nature bring us this message once a year.

    I finally understand this changing the colors is God's way of telling us once we pass, life does continue in all its glory with beauty. We should not fear death, nor should we feel that it's final. We will continue in his beautiful reflection after our time here is over. We will be here just in a different realm to support and watch out for our loved ones who remain here for the time being until the time comes for them to call us by their side.

    The next time you look at the beauty the trees bring us in their annual glorious show believe in the message of how beautiful life is here and when we pass the beauty continues.

Regret

    You should never regret not having done something in your life. If you didn't do something you wished you had, it wasn't right for you at the time. It wasn't meant to be. Let it go. By holding onto regret, you will lose time when you could have been doing something more productive with your life, not to mention enjoying life as you should and as you can; if you only let yourself.

    I view living with regret like riding a stationary bike. (I'm not talking health benefits now, I'm not going that deep here. It's just an analogy, okay. So stay with me.) You pedal hard and fast, exerting high levels of energy, but at the end of that trip, you are in the same place you started.

    Everything looks the same there. You simply get on every day to accomplish nothing and do not find anything worthwhile. No, you are stuck there. You're not going forward. Hell, not even sideways. You're just stuck using all that energy. The benefit is limited. When you live with regret or in the past, you are always just there in that same place.

    Get off that bike (regret), leave that room behind, and live every day as it is meant to be; a new experience, a fresh look at the day. Have fun, laugh, and breathe the fresh new air. Not the still stale air of that room you are stuck in.

You will see colors and feel again. The new life without regret will be wonderful and you'll find you can take control of your life and make things happen; maybe not just for you but others in your life.

When you start this new journey, be patient, It may take a while, but if you're persistent, you can make it happen. As the light shines upon your life and you feel how good life without regret is, you will cross that line and never go back. Never look back. There is no reason to.

When you live with regret it colors your whole world, whether you realize it or not.

Projection

Projection is constructive when it comes to business; an important element for the health and future of the company. Businesses can control this with the right team and realistic goals that are often met or exceeded. But this is not about business, it's about your personal life.

When it comes to our personal life, projecting is destructive. We sit looking, guessing (projecting) our future with our eyes of today and how we see it. When we do project our vision, in this case, it is hard and fast. This is what is going to happen and something will make it happen. The fact is our eyes are incapable of seeing the future. So what does projecting actually do for you?

As I see it, we project in one of two ways, which can be, and often are, destructive. This is the reason projecting sets you up for a letdown.

1 - If you look at the future with rose-colored glasses and are expecting wonderful things to happen, you will be depressed or greatly disappointed if they don't happen as we projected. Those of us who do that more often than not, have our expectations set far above attainable goals and when it doesn't happen we are let down. Many will be so sure something great is going to happen that they sit back and wait. This is a catastrophic waste of time.

2 - I will call, 'it's never going to happen,' the worst of them both. They are negative or it's going to be bad. It often keeps you stuck and we refuse to try anything at all. I call it the 'why should we,' it's always bad. That is without a doubt the most destructive. It's inevitable. We will sink into a depressed state for more often than not for no reason. This attitude will prevent one from even trying to make their life better. No one can see how things will be or how they will turn out.

Do not mistake goals for projection. I have addressed projection above. We can set goals as long as they are attainable. As we work toward our goals and do not expect them to happen, when things do not go as planned, we can do what I call 'dance.' We can always find a way. As long as we stay hopeful, never hopeless.

Projecting is expecting something to happen. Goals are making something you want to happen, set goals and work toward them so you can do it.

Value

When I was young, at an age I can barely remember, my dad was an assistant conductor on the New York Central Railroad. He would bring me small thoughtful gifts; gifts of real life. Not toys or clothing. Nothing materialistic. These gifts were items from his job, such as colored tickets used to indicate a passenger on the train had paid. I loved collecting all the colors. One gift he brought me, which to this day, sits fondly in my memory, is a railroad SPIKE.

This large nail-like object is used to hold the rail to the tie (large wood that goes under the rail), keeping the tracks in place. The spikes would vibrate out occasionally as the steam engines rumbled by. It would just lay on the ground when it came out; seemingly awaiting a caring home.

Dad would pick one up on occasion, wrap in a white piece of paper and bring it home to me. A special meaningful gift. It was like getting gold. It was never about the monetary value. This rusty old spike is of priceless value which I treasure to this day.

What value could anyone place on the simple act of the thoughtfulness a father has for his child?

This is About You and No One Else

It's About Love & Hate

This is not about the election or what happened. I use this as an example of how we allow situations which are out of our control to take control over our lives.

Love

I am watching the losing side get very depressed even though nothing has been officially resolved. Yet they are worried about their future and the future of this country. They have given up. They are allowing things that are out of their control to get to them. They must learn that no matter what happens, and we seriously do not know yet, they will have to make the most of their life and not let any situation take them down. They must simply wait for any situation out to the end. This group looks at all sides before they make up their minds.

Hate

The other side of this is the in-your-face poor sports, again nothing has been finalized but they have jumped on this to get into the face of the loser. They have let hate take them over. I will throw in anger as well. No matter what happens they have done enormous damage to their image and integrity. This is an example of how we allow our hate to control us without giving any thought to how we look to others and how damaging that is. This group doesn't look at all sides just find something or someone to hate. Hate blinds us and anger shuts us out.

Once we allow this to happen, we are finished. We have shown all those around us that winning is more important than our integrity and creditability. Those around us quickly realize we have no confidence in ourselves and live superficial life through outside situations that are out of our control. It is the more damaging of the two. It will cost you both relationships and employment opportunities.

I have said it over a hundred times I'm sure — never let your hate and anger define who you are — work on it. You will be happy you did.

As for the first group, learn to let any situation play out before you give up. Show strength and resolve. You will be better off.

Remember we can overcome most things in life once we set our minds to it.

Never Give Up. Never, Never Give Up…
I paraphrase Winston Churchill.

The Life of a Caulbearer

The House Clearing

I received a text from Jane, a client from the past. She asked what dates I had open and wanted to book an appointment for her daughter. Her daughter Judy, wasn't ready when I saw her.

We set it up for the following Tuesday. I remembered Jane but not her house or what our session was about. My memories of sessions are fleeting; which is a good thing. You see, basically I am lazy, and knowing me, I would be tempted to take the easy road and just repeat what I told you the last time. However, I could never do that as I wouldn't be able to live with myself.

As I arrived at the house for Judy's session, I remembered the house, nothing more. It wasn't until I stepped into the house that I felt the energy. After we finished Judy's session, she and I spoke about the last time I was there. She reminded me that I did a clearing when I was there.

I remembered sitting in the living room. I told her mom, Jane, about a Christmas party. I told her there was a tree in front of the doors and there was a piano being played by one of the family. Judy confirmed a piano that was played by a family member. She also told me they did put the tree in the place where the doors are. At the time this Christmas would have taken place, the doors were not in use like they are today. Christmas was an important celebration for the original family.

I saw the souls walking around the house and doing a harvest in the fall. It turned out the house was a farmhouse that overlooked a large apple orchard. The fall crop was apples; which was a big event for the family that originally owned the house and land. It was their business, although the family was a prominent family in Peekskill.

Jane told me she was bothered by all the activity. I told her I would ask them to leave. I sat concentrated and gathered them together. I told them it was time to leave the house and give Jane some peace. They agreed and told me they would just come back for the harvest. I told them the orchards were gone. But not to them, so they were insisting they stay for harvest. I asked them to please leave again which they once again agreed to.

I hadn't heard if anything happened until I did Judy's session. She told me the activity slowed down. I was getting that some of them came back in the fall. That was when there is activity in the house.

Judy filled me in on how things went right after I left that day. She told me the activity stopped in the house for some time. There is still a little activity from time to time but it didn't make her nervous. I got that it wasn't the family that owned the house. I told Judy it was from her mom. Mom and the activity was mostly in the kitchen where we were sitting. Judy confirmed that. I also got a man outside working in the garden. It was her grandfather who loved to garden. Judy also confirmed that. I let both her and Jane know that it was just their family watching over them. 98% of the time, activity in a house is one of our loved ones.

When I Don't Hear a Word

Things are not the same on the other side as they are here. Most people who come to me believe the messages they receive however, once in a while, a client will test me and the souls. They will ask me to give them a phrase or one word the person on the other side would use when they were here or they had a pact that they would say it on the other side. I often hear those before I am asked. I will say something and my client will tell me that is exactly what the souls with us would say.

The souls do not like to be challenged; whether you believe in them or not. When people do this, they slow the messages because the souls do not want to use their energy being questioned and being doubted. They tell me what they want my client to hear, not necessarily what clients wants to hear. I explain that to everyone in my intro prior to starting a session.

I recently did a session with a family who lost their father. I sat with his widow, Mary, and their two sons, Roger and Dennis. They validated everything I told the sons. However, Mom wanted to know the word she and her husband agreed to say if they spoke to someone like me. That isn't something I often get and when someone asks, I want to give the what they need.

What will happen in that case, logic will begin to seep into my zone. When that happens it's over. It takes me out of my zone. I will tell my client I will continue to concentrate on what they are looking for over the next few days.

In this particular case, the very next day I heard several things that made no sense. All but one thing that was meaningful for Mary's daughter-in-law. Her sons told me she was disappointed because of it. Roger and Dennis received most of the messages during that session. I was never able to connect with that word. I have realized that sometimes the souls just don't remember and this type of validation is disrespectful to them even though they understand the people they left behind really want to hear something so they can believe I am really connected with their loved ones. Sadly, they discount everything else they hear, no matter how meaningful it was, simply because of that.

Not to long after that session, I was doing a session with another client. When we finished our session, we were talking. I was telling her about that session and what happened with the word thing when she said, "You *did* get that connection for me."

I asked her what the word was and she told me it wasn't a word. Instead, it was when her husband did a crazy clog dance. He told her he would do his dance for her. That made me realize my clients are getting what they look for in some way that will often not make sense to me.

I now ask my clients to be open and receptive to all messages. Listen to what the souls are telling them, and what they need will be there for them.

Never Hold onto the Past

After years of doing sessions, I have become aware that people living in the past often struggle with depression. It may be our overall greater past in general or something more specific we have done and just can't let go of, no matter how trivial or severe. This is something that should be addressed by mental health experts if it isn't already.

I am realizing more and more that holding onto the past is detrimental to one's mental health. Many people struggle with some form of depression. I am not talking about bipolar disorder or clinical depression. It's more what I call environmental or perhaps situational depression. Hell, I'm no doctor, so I'm not sure what the scientific definition is. I hope I make sense here, so stay with me.

During the sessions, when I see my client is depressed, one of the souls will bring up a situation my client can't move beyond. The souls, through me, tell my client they have to let go. They show the path to a better life by letting the past go.

Youth is often the culprit. Yes, youth. We do stupid things we were not proud of when we were kids. We all have. Hell, if I hung onto the stupid things I'm not proud of doing as a kid, I would end up being referred to a doctor with a very thick prescription pad who would send me on a trip to the Rainbow Room with a closet full of medication. I, like many, was young and stupid. Maybe I still am (not young.)

The past we are holding onto cannot be changed, nor will it change. There is absolutely nothing we can do about our past except learn the lessons we were meant to learn.

We also can't fix what we went through. No one can. We should never allow anything from yesterday to have so much control over us today. It takes us down. When we realize this, we are able to stop giving 'the past' power over us. That is when we can walk away from depression.

Never beat yourself up over anything you can't change; especially the past.

As I was cleaning off my desk... Okay, to be honest, the papers were piled so high that they all fell off! LOL!

Anyway, I found this saying that I printed out from someone. I forget who it was or I would give them credit. To me, this is one of the most important keys to moving toward and finding a happier life. It sums what I wrote above in one sentence.

"You can't start the next chapter of your life if you keep reading the last one!"

Let that sink in and take that advice.

Myths

Because there is no science, studies, or proof, what many mediums tell their clients is based on theories; not studies or even logic. The information is parroted from one Provider to the next. Many believe it sounds good and adopt it without thinking and rarely apply logic to these theories.

Yes, many things have happened to me that are unexplained, such as phones acting up or texts coming from nowhere. Some make sense while others don't. Other times there are voices between myself and my client while on the phone. I have also experienced animals and birds acting up or lights going on and off.

Sage burning, or smudging, is a sacred practice that can be traced back through many cultures over thousands of years. The idea is that the smoke is purifying because it captures the "bad energy" and then "ascends to the heavens." Incense or herbal smoke is most commonly used – be it by Buddhists, Catholics, Maoris, or Native Americans.

But I question this. Why? Think about this: What prevents a smoke that can capture bad energy from capturing good energy? Apply some logical critical thinking.

Crystals are another thing I question. I have been given many crystals which I am told will serve a purpose like finding love or money. However, none have ever done anything the claims say it will.

I also hear other things that I find amazing. For example, I hear we must wait at least one year after a person passes before they will come to us. There are a few reasons given. Such as, they need to rest or recover from this life.

Souls have come to me as soon as a week after or even the same day they have passed. I believe this is spread around so that television personalities can do a search on the client to see who passed and any circumstances of their passing. If someone tells you this move away from them. In my opinion, they are not real.

On occasion, I have also been told by clients, that their spouse doesn't want me to come to their house. The reason is that they believe I will bring "spirits" with me and they will stay after I leave. Ahh nooo. The truth is, the souls are there when I get there and stay when I leave. The souls are the people who were once here for you. They watch over you and help you get through things. They bring me to the clients in many ways; mostly through referrals or sometimes the person will just show up at a place where I am for no apparent or explainable reason. The souls bring that person to me so they can hear messages.

I never advertise,. It's like, 'Poof! Here I am.'

Neither of us know why until the messages they were meant to hear have been received.

If you test the souls, they don't like that. They will give you enough proof and expect you to accept that. After our session, my client will know exactly who the souls who are with us are. The more you test them the less they are there for us. You are asking them to use more energy than is necessary. They want you to believe in them.

They are not guardian angels, they are souls. They do watch out for us, but they are no angels.

I also had a few people tell me not to do readings when they are pregnant. What?!? Seriously, I have done many sessions with pregnant women over the years and they all delivered healthy babies with no complications.

I have no idea why many mediums or "psychics" do that, but don't be gullible. Question everything and never, never tell a medium anything until you are sure they are real.

These are just a few things to watch for when dealing with practitioners in this modality who claim they have the gift. As you can tell by now, I live in the logical world. My clients must hear the messages they need to hear, not what I believe they want to hear or some 'hocus pocus' that may sound good, but will not make sense.

Again, practitioners who ask you lots of questions then tell you what you want to hear are not real. Question everything when it comes to this.

Finally, the practitioner either hears the voices or not. You can't take classes or study under anyone. I see them in a faded, black and white movie. They speak to me in whispers. I firmly believe God grants those of us who are genuine the ability to hear and see the souls. I simply relay the messages to my client from the souls in the movie.

I never get dark messages. When I hear others give dark messages, I believe they are not real. The souls don't come with dark messages, but that is an article for another time.

I stay grounded to help ground my clients. I thank God every day for the ability he has granted me to help others. The best way to describe who I am and how I work is simply put: "I do not live in rainbow town on a unicorn farm with a crystal garden."

The Souls Find Me When They Need to Send a Message

I can't begin to tell you how often I am working somewhere and someone will come in and express to me they felt they had to come in but don't know why.

Yeah, that happens to me too — when I go into the kitchen and can't remember why I went there! LOL! But that isn't what I am talking about.

I have had, on several occasions, someone walk into a store where I was working and say they saw the sign on the building and had a feeling they needed to come in.

One time, a woman came in and was confused as to why she was there and expressed that to the owner. As she was talking to the owner, a woman came to me telling me that she needed to find her passion (see page 75 in my book *They Speak Through Me: Messages From Beyond*).

I have recently begun to do TikTok posts. I did a video on how we shouldn't judge everything by the way it is today and worry things will never change. The truth is things are always changing and we do have control over our lives. It is up to us to bring about the change we need in our lives.

Several hours after I did that post, one of my clients Tina saw it and it resonated with her. Now like going into the kitchen and forgetting why I was there, I rarely remember the sessions I give. I will remember bits and pieces, but not the whole thing. They come through me and don't stay with me. The souls do that so I don't get stuck on something and listen to all the messages they are about to bring to my client.

Tina was stuck and couldn't seem to move on. She was feeling things were never going to change for her. So she felt the need to reach out to me for another session. Her messages were what she needed. She told me they gave her hope and the strength to move forward.

This is what I do. It is my calling. I help guide my client through messages from the souls. They direct me on what my client needs. I do not control them. I tell people when we start, the souls will tell you what *they* want you to hear, not what you want to hear. If you want to hear what you want to hear, go drinking with a buddy. I'm not your guide and I honor that.

Red Spotted Ambassador

As soon as I stepped on my front door today, I noticed a Red Spotted Ambassador butterfly just sitting there on my step. It didn't move at all. And although they are common, this was my first time seeing one.

I noticed how beautiful this butterfly was; in all its Glory. The beautiful colors brought my attention to it. I wanted to capture a photo of this beauty. I ran back into the house to get my camera. Knowing how butterflies don't stay in one place for long, I fully expected the little guy to be gone. However, when I returned, it was still sitting right where it was.

I was able to get a few shots when it flew to a stone right by where it was sitting. I grabbed a few more shots before I had to leave. I knew the way it was acting that this had to be a sign. It wasn't acting as normal butterflies do. I would have to concentrate on this later as I had to run to see JoAnn and Mary whose young family member, Andrea, was found dead a few days ago.

While I was with JoAnn and Mary, the woman's boyfriend, Leon, was there as well. He was suspected of hurting Andrea by the family but I was getting that he didn't do it. What I *was* getting was Andrea choking along with hitting her head. I felt it was a suicide and that she took pills causing her to choke, fall, and hit her head.

As I was talking to the boyfriend, his dad came to me. I began to tell him about his dad. I had no idea if his dad was passed but this soul was strong and when I described him and what he was like, Leon broke down and began to cry. He pulled a flyer and card from his pocket from his dad's wake, which he carries around with him. His dad meant a lot to him and he got the messages he needed. He was told that he needs to get his act together. This was up to him. All I can do is deliver the message with the hopes he takes the journey.

I didn't notice what was going on around Leon as I was giving him his messages; mainly because I go into a zone and close my eyes while doing a session. A small butterfly was flying all around him and landed on his head at one point. The family members watched that little guy as it flew around.

While I was giving Leon his messages, I realized the butterfly this morning was brought by Andrea to thank me for what I was doing for the family. After I finished the messages with Leon, I told the family about the butterfly on my step earlier and I believed it was Andrea who brought it to us.

I showed JoAnn and Mary the photos of the Red Spotted Ambassador which I took earlier. They appeared to be surprised. When I asked them what was happening, they told me a Red Spotted Ambassador was flying around Leon while I was giving him his messages. My confirmation that it was Andrea. They told me a story about how Andrea was afraid of butterflies and they used to chase her with butterflies when she was a little kid. They said they teased her recently about her fear of them.

Andrea is no longer afraid of butterflies and the little beauties are all around her to give her joy in heaven. She wanted to share that joy with JoAnn and Mary.

Wayne's Influence

I had diverticulosis and was slated for surgery when a friend introduced me to Wayne Gabari and Kathy Raymond. They are transformational healers. When my friend told me about them, I had no idea what energy healing was. I never heard of anything like this before my friend mentioned it.

Upon reaching out to Wayne, we decided to meet at my house for the healing. At the beginning of my massage, while on the table, I was thinking, "Here I am getting a massage from a guy without a happy ending."

(Not that I would want a happy ending from a guy, but I digress.)

It wasn't long before I was out in what I could best describe as a twilight state.

Wayne's healing worked. I was still in the medical model and I was skeptical to say the least, but all the pain I was experiencing was gone. A little over a week later I went to the doctor's ordered colonoscopy. After the colonoscopy, the doctor told me there were some diverticula but it was healed. This was just what I needed to help me believe in Wayne's healing.

I sent everyone I knew to both Wayne and his partner Kathy. When a friend of mine's two-year-old grandson had rare brain cancer, I told my friend about

Wayne. I asked him if the family would consider a healing from Wayne. The family agreed and I took Wayne to the little boy's house to do the healing. As I was sitting in the dining room waiting for them to finish the healing in the child's bedroom, I was having visions of Jesus.

Now, as a cop, whenever people saw Jesus or believed they were Jesus, it always required a ride to the rainbow room (also known as the psych hospital.) I was also thinking, and I had no idea why at the time, that the father was in the room thinking about a business meeting.

Here I am worried about having to head off to that wondrous destination filled with meds and straitjackets, when my 'thoughts' went to the father having a business meeting. I had no idea why I was thinking about any of those things; the business meeting or the visions of Jesus.

They came out of the healing and Wayne told the family he asked several Divine Spirits to come to help him during the healing; including Jesus.

I'm thinking, "Okay, that explains the vision."

I was a bit relieved. My visit to the rainbow room could be put off for now.

Then the father told Wayne he was sorry for not being present while in the room. He was thinking about a business meeting he had coming up Monday. I almost fell off my chair wondering where the hell all this came from.

As we were finishing and getting ready to leave, I was talking to the boy's mother. I was telling her things that made no sense to me yet made perfect sense to her. I had no idea where her message was coming from but I did tell her we should talk more which, unfortunately, never happened.

That was one of the most confusing days of my life, and trust me, I have had more than my fair share of confusing days. Hell, it's been a confusing life in general.

I wrote in my first book, *They Speak Through Me: Messages from Beyond*, (page 9) about my argument with

Sheri, a medium who Wayne called as we were driving home, to see if she could see how the healing went.

Essentially, she told me I had to do this. I told her I couldn't. Sheri was ultimately right and here I am doing sessions for people for over fourteen years.

The little boy lived cancer-free for about a year living longer than expected.

This event was the beginning of my Journey as a Caulbearer.

Catherine

As time went by and my gifts as a caulbearer grew, my healer friend Wayne would occasionally ask me how his healing was going. One such event was his work on Catherine. Catherine had stage four cancer throughout her body.

Wayne would ask me what I saw with her healing. I always gave him what I was getting for her until one day I advised hi that I should talk to her directly. Catherine was very skeptical of what I do and this whole process; especially what I do. However, Wayne was able to convince her because the messages he had received from me were so accurate.

Catherine eventually agreed to meet with me; skeptical as she was. We met at her home in Manhattan in October. Her physicians told her she would most likely not see Christmas. Perhaps, if she was lucky, she might make it to January.

Once I got into my zone, Catherine's father, with whom she was very close, came through. I was in the process of telling Catherine how she would be at peace and not struggling when all of a sudden, I said, "You will be cancer-free by February."

I was not just shocked at what came out of my mouth, but was mortified I would say such a thing. I apologized to her I didn't want to give her false hopes. She understood and our session continued. All of her messages from that day on were about her getting better.

Christmas came and went and she was still alive. We continued to talk on the phone for weeks. She was happy. However, she remained cautiously optimistic.

At the beginning of February, Catherine called to tell me the cat scan showed three cancerous nodules in her stomach. I had a vision of them vaporizing and they weren't there. I advised her of this but also told her that I saw something on her liver. She said the doctors didn't see it.

Two days later she called me and told me they found cancer on her liver. I told her I found it, not the doctors, and what I saw was a cyst holding poison, not cancer. At the end of February, Catherine went for surgery to remove the three nodules they saw in her stomach. I reminded her of what I saw, but I could not, nor would I tell her, not to go for the surgery. She did the surgery at the end of February.

Catherine called me at the beginning of March, with the results of her surgery. No cancer and the cyst on her liver was holding dead cancer cells. Everything I told her proved right.

Catherine lived another three years before her cancer came back. Two weeks before she called me to tell me this, I knew it was back. When she called, I was so taken aback as my vision was right.

Sadly, Catherine told me she had given up on the healings and was putting her faith in alternative liquids. I tried to convince her to get back to Wayne's healings but being in that medical model she felt the liquid she was taking was the reason her cancer went away in the first place. It was also apparent to me that her will to live was just not there any longer. This necessary to help us to continue on. It was not long after our conversation that Catherine passed away.

Catherine's story was amazing, it was my first serious session. To this day, I continue to be amazed at what I got for her.

I know Catherine is now whole and happy and is with her dad.

Wayne Asked Me About His Friend

I received a call from my friend and transformational healer, Wayne Gabari. He asked me if I could get something on his friend Richie who passed. Wayne advised me he is in touch with Richie's friend Kathy who lived with him in his house. Wayne told me she felt something move by her and asked if I could get anything on it. I told him I will have to call him back.

The next day I called Wayne to tell him Richie told me he used to tickle Kathy's feet while they sat on the couch. Wayne called me back and she confirmed that happened often. They would be sitting on the couch watching television and he would do that.

Kathy was made the executor of Richie's will and was getting a lot of pushback from Richie's two daughters. They were estranged from Richie and had nothing to do with him for years.

Although they were left out of the will on purpose, they were contesting it. Kathy was concerned about this because the will allowed her to be able to live in the house for the next ten years. But the daughters wanted her out. They wanted to take the house and property which Richie shared with his brother.

I got that the daughters are wasting their time. This turned out to be true.

Wayne brought me to Kathy's house a few weeks later to meet her. I wasn't expecting to do a session. It was just a meet and greet. But when I was standing there with Kathy, her parents came through as well as her grandmother. She received messages that were important for her to hear; how her mother was proud she came through the troubled waters she had negotiated most of her life.

Then Richie came through. He told her she had something coming at her from the family within the next few days. He told her to have confidence in herself and stand strong no matter what.

Three days later, Wayne calls me to tell me that Kathy got a call informing her that the daughters planned to contest the will. I believe they wanted her to cave. She didn't. She stuck to her guns and they were shot down, no pun intended. (Richie was a gun guy. That is likely why that sentence just came out of me.)

Kathy and I discussed getting together when she had time to do a proper session rather than a short impromptu session. That not only shocked her, but surprised me as well.

When we were finished, I was outside saying goodbye to Wayne and Kathy. If you know me, my goodbyes can take longer than a session! Yes, as my wife says, I am a marathon mouth. I don't know when to shut up.

All of a sudden as I was walking to my car, I saw Richie doing a funny dance. I turned to Kathy and told her, "Richie is doing an Irish Jig."

She laughed. She said he did that all the time at parties and other gatherings. When she heard that, she was relieved to know he is in a good place now. He had lost his ability to move toward the end of his life. I advised her that he was doing that to let her know he was whole now and that he still has his sense of humor.

With respect to me not being able to find my keys, Kathy asked me if I knew where Richie's .32 caliber Gun was.

Richie said, "Mattress."

We went and checked his mattress. Nope, not there. Then he said, "Drawer." Not there either.

He was screwing with me. I believe that was his nature. I'm sure that gun will show up at some time.

No Effect on Me

I discovered one day, that little happens to me during a session that has any effect on me. It was just another interesting session. I have written about many of these unique situations, such as lights going on or off, a hummingbird coming right up to me while on the phone talking to a client, a red fox screaming in my backyard then it walking off quietly once the message is relayed to the client I was talking to at that time, and many more.

I realized this when a client said to me how cool it is that the situations happen to me; which is not frequent. The truth is, I just don't think about them. Yes, I write about them, but not because I feel it's cool or whatever. I enjoy these events, but it's like, 'Okay, that was interesting.'

I write about them for two reasons. One is to let people know what I do and what I get so if someone is looking, or better yet, needs to find someone like me, they will reach out. The other reason is that I need to clear up what happened and make sense of strange happenings in my head. Before I accept one of these strange events, I look at every logical angle. Once it is clear there is no way that should have happened, I go back into my zone and ask who just did that. It's always a relative or loved one when it happens during a session.

People are conditioned by the entertainment world that there are evil spirits around. When things happen in someone's home, like something moving or a light going on, they worry something bad is going to happen or something is haunting their house. I assure you, it is just some mischievous souls who is looking for attention and want you to know they are there for you.

Every so often it's not a soul that you know but someone who lived in the house or in the area that stayed and finds its way to you. I had one such situation where a little boy was in a house and was communicating with one of the children telling him to do crazy things.

That little boy was that way when he was here. I told the child to leave the house and that he wasn't welcome. The homeowner told me he left for a while but came back. I wonder if the child returned or if the homeowner used the haunting for attention. Not everything you hear about houses having spirits actually has spirits. I think sometimes people make it up for attention.

Old Common Phrases

There are times when I hear a common phrase from the souls but I do not say it. This is in reaction to the skeptics who are always trying to prove us to be fake by suggesting that everyone would use that phrase. So I push the souls a little harder for something different.

Because it is important to me that my client believes the healing messages they bring to us, I worry they may think I'm talking in platitudes. So I would hesitate to say a common phrase. That being said, I am realizing now that I need to say whatever phrase I get. It took me a while to get it, but I am there now.

Just the other day during a session a mother, Wilma, used an old phrase. She told Sara her daughter that if she didn't wake up, she would, "knock her into next Tuesday."

I didn't say it at first, but mom kept saying it so I figured I better say it before Wilma knocked me into next Tuesday. I finally told Sara what her mother was saying. She laughed and told me that was one of her mother's favorite terms. It was very meaningful for Sara to hear it.

My lesson: just because it is a commonly used phrase, doesn't mean the soul with me didn't use it and probably did use it often.

During another session, I told my client, Carol that her dad had a hat on. Honestly, I very rarely see men wearing hats. Hell, women either, for that matter.

When I told her that her dad was wearing a hat, she told me all men wore hats back then. This was about the fifth time Carol said that to me about a message I was giving her. Carol's husband was a retired cop. He told her to expect me to tell her common things.

I finally stopped her at that point and said, "We are the same age and I come from a big Italian family, none of the men in the family wore hats. So no, that isn't true. As she received several other messages, she stopped doing that realizing what I was getting couldn't be put into that narrow-minded box. As we were ending, Carol asked for her cousin who hadn't come through.

I told her I had a woman coming through with red hair; a wild woman, fun and funny. I received messages about some of the things they did together. She confirmed it was her cousin. At that point, I asked Carol if I could ask her a question. She said sure. I asked Carol if all her cousins were like that.

She smiled and said, "I get it."

When the souls give me messages, I have to go with what they are saying and tell my clients no matter what. Whether it makes sense or not, it always does.

He Googled Me

Let me put people interested in doing a session at ease, I never Google people except in the spirit world by talking to their friends and relatives who have passed.

No, I simply do not have time to answer twenty to thirty emails a day, average three sessions a day and attempt to write and finish books — then somehow find the time to Google someone.

I never google people not on this side of the veil. My Google search comes through the spirit world by talking to their relatives.

Yes, that's right Heaven is my Google search. I also don't use Duck Duck Go or any other search engine for my sessions. It's strictly Heaven.

Dad Thought I Googled Him

I did a session with a man who lost his son with whom he had been close (see happy Birthday pop). He was referred to me by a friend. After our session, he indicated he was very happy but seem to have a little uncertainty.

A few days later I got a call from the woman who referred me and she told me he was very happy but questioned whether or not I had Googled him. She asked him if he gave me his last name. He told her he hadn't. That is when he realized that this was all real. You can't Google someone without a last name. Having that trust has made our growing relationship strong.

John and Joan

I had a man named John call for a session one day. I asked how he found me. He didn't want to say. I told John that I was just trying to track how people found me. He said he was referred. I asked him by who. He didn't want to tell me.

Christ, it's like you are living the same life as the person who referred me I thought. But, I behaved myself, somehow, and didn't say that to John out loud.

Okay, so we get past that and I let it go because I most likely wouldn't remember that person anyway and I didn't want it to cause any issues with the session.

The session was great. John was a dentist and he worked with his dad who came through. I also got that he has issues with relationships. It seems the souls that were there for him felt he was difficult; something I was beginning to see on my own.

John challenged me at every point during the session until I explained exactly what I was getting in great detail. John couldn't seem to grasp what he was getting from his souls, which at that point, he did finally acknowledged made sense.

I had to work hard for him to understand what it was I was hearing. As he was doing this, it was slowing the messages I was hearing down and the souls were getting agitated with him. My experience is the more you challenge the souls the fewer messages they will give me. In Johns's case, I even had one soul in particular who was standing in the background but hadn't come forward and didn't seem to want to.

As the messages ended, I asked John if there was someone he wanted to hear from who hadn't come through. I said that he should give me their first name only.

He asked for Joan. Once he said her name, the woman in the back came forward. I told him I have a tall, quiet redhead with me. I continued to give him additional information about her as she gave it to me. I asked if that was her and he said, "Yes."

As it turned out, she was the one I wasn't able to identify who was sitting back in the background. I told him that she was here. As I continued to describe her to him, he said acknowledged it is her.

Sadly, before I could finish, John began yelling.

"She didn't come through on her own! That means she doesn't want to talk to me! So, I don't want to hear from her!"

I attempted to explain to him there are times when the souls want to be asked for; for many reasons. Some reasons are that they feel they don't want to upset my client, so they wait until they feel the client is ready to hear from them or they just want to feel wanted.

But John didn't want to talk to her no matter what I said. So I ended the session.

As we ended the session, John said in an extremely abusive way, "Thanks for not Googling me!"

It was abundantly clear that he was having difficulty as a "man of science" believing his messages and because the messages were right, I *must* have Googled him.

Of course, I didn't. I couldn't. I didn't even know his last name.

Wellllllll, John paid via PayPal at the end of the session. This meant his full name was there.

So you know what I did? Yes you do.

I Googled him!

After about an hour of searching, the only

thing I was able to find out was that he was a dentist who was in practice with his dad. But nothing else. More came through during our session.

Think About This

As I said earlier, I do not have time to do a Google search on any client much less every client. I understand there is speculation that television mediums do have people checked out. Why would anyone do this? It's simple. Because they feel they must be right. It's all show for them and very important for their ratings.

Don't get me wrong. It's important for me to be right as well. So what is the difference?

I have faith in the gifts God granted me. I know that as long as the reason for anyone doing this is pure, the messages will always come from the souls that are there for my clients.

If I did a background check on anyone and repeated what I found out, I couldn't live with myself. When clients contact me for a session, I ask them to not tell me anything about themselves. Also, any questions I ask please just say, 'yes, no, or maybe.' Please do not expand further than that.

If I did Google my clients, I would lose all creditability. I would never be able to get it back no matter what I did. But that isn't my primary concern. My *primary* concern is that I never want to hurt anyone.

Clients who come to me are in pain. They are with me looking for closure. It would be devastating for them to think this isn't real. I take that seriously and go the extra mile to make sure it is about my client and getting the messages they need.

One of my clients who lost her 6-year-old son went to a well-known television medium with her family. She had told the medium's producer her life story. The medium called her two days later and repeated back what she told the producer.

They realized quickly that they knew there was nothing said by that medium during their "reading" she that didn't already know.

Because of this, the father felt there is no such thing as an afterlife and he would never see his son again. He was so angry. They are now divorced and he has been arrested for violence.

What she did to them is unforgivable and devastating. I made a promise to myself that I would never be that person. If for some reason God took my gifts away, I would just stop doing this instead of faking it.

Sadly, many mediums feel they have to be right and slam it during a "reading". They make it about themselves, not their clients. They let their ego get in the way of doing what is right for others. I am also coming to a realization, having been around many of them, that there may be some psychological issues involved as well.

With all that being said, think about this above all. What would I find out about you if I did Google you? How important are you that you or anyone would believe their entire life is on Google? Let's for argument's sake say I am doing someone famous or their family member (and I have). What would I find if I did a search on that famous person?

What I would actually get on someone famous are press releases from their public relations team or things put up by others trying to tear them down. Long story short, what you will find on a search is basic stuff controlled by the famous and nothing extraordinary on the average John Q citizen.

Have you ever tried to Google someone who isn't well known? Waste of time.

Try it. Try doing a search on yourself and see what comes up. Don't be too disappointed when you discover your life's history isn't on there.

If you have ever had a session with me, you'd see

that almost nothing I told you is on Google. No folks the souls don't use Google; they just whisper in my ear important information their loved ones need at that time.

I trust the souls. They will bring me information that no one could find on any type of search.

Trust the messages, I do.

About the Author

Born with a veil on his face, a sign of psychic abilities, Bob understood from a very early age he was different. At the age of 8 Bob began to see strong visions of the future and of things to come. Not understanding exactly what was happening, Bob ignored them, thinking it was simply his imagination. As he grew older they were more timely. He knew within a half hour when something was going to happen, but continued to ignore the messages until recently, when he began to receive strong messages and visions from beyond for others.

Bob receives calls worldwide, as well as all from over the country and Canada. His clients come to him almost exclusively through referrals. Loved ones or souls for others come from beyond to Bob no matter where he is. Bob will tell you that the messages come for people sitting next to him or walking by. "I never know when they will come, they just find me."

When bob does a session, he always gets messages from beyond that are positive. Bob never asks his clients questions, nor will he allow them to give him any information until it's established who is coming through and why they are here.

The messages are uplifting and healing for those receiving them. Bob considers himself a healer as much as a Caulbearer. He is thankful for his gifts which allow him to help others in a time of need.

Contact: 914.879.1115
Bbucha3458@aol.com

For more information visit:
www.bobbcaulmedium.com

or on Facebook
www.facebook.com/bobbmedium

www.ingramcontent.com/pod-product-compliance
Lightning Source LLC
Chambersburg PA
CBHW050650160426
43194CB00010B/1885